Daily *warm-ups*

SHAKESPEARE

J. WESTON
WALCH
PUBLISHER
Portland, Maine

Special thanks to the following editors who helped make this book possible:

Susan Blair, Maggie Jones, Holly Moirs, Mary Rich, and Erica Varney

1 2 3 4 5 6 7 8 9 10

ISBN 0-8251-4483-3

Copyright © 2003
J. Weston Walch, Publisher
P.O. Box 658 • Portland, Maine 04104-0658
www.walch.com

Printed in the United States of America

Table of Contents

iii

The *Daily Warm-Ups* series is a wonderful way to turn extra classroom minutes into valuable learning time. The 180 quick activities—one for each day of the school year—introduce students to Shakespeare and his works. These daily activities may be used at the very beginning of class to get students into learning mode, near the end of class to make good educational use of that transitional time, in the middle of class to shift gears between lessons—or whenever else you have minutes that now go unused. In addition to providing students with structure and focus, they are a natural path to other language arts activities.

Daily Warm-Ups are easy-to-use reproducibles—simply photocopy the day's activity and distribute it. Or make a transparency of the activity and project it on the board. You may want to use the activities for extra credit points or as a method of prompting classroom discussion.

The first half of the book addresses background, history, technique, and themes. The latter half helps develop students' ability to interpret Shakespeare's words through direct quotations from his plays.

However you choose to use them, *Daily Warm-Ups* are a convenient and useful supplement to your regular lesson plans. Make every minute of your class time count!

William Shakespeare's plays feature sexual situations and references, violence, gore, and profanity. His plays are widely taught in schools throughout the country. Many movies made today have the same features.

Why do you think you are restricted from attending movies with these features but you can read Shakespeare's plays in school?

William Shakespeare had to draw an audience for his plays. He chose the titles so that people would know what to expect. He wrote three types of plays: comedies, tragedies, and histories.

Based on the title or what you may already know about the play, match each title below to its type and briefly explain your choices.

_____ 1. *As You Like It*   a. tragedy

_____ 2. *Romeo and Juliet*   b. history

_____ 3. *King Richard III*   c. comedy

2

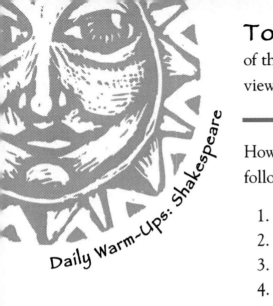

Today we consider Shakespeare the greatest writer of the English language. In his own lifetime he might have been viewed differently.

How might he have been described then? Select one of the following choices and explain your answer.

1. Most popular actor
2. Best playwright
3. Best poet
4. Queen Elizabeth's favorite playwright
5. Most popular entertainer

Shakespeare's plays were each more than two hours long. Each had a main story line, or plot, and other less important stories or subplots. Today, television sitcoms are less than a half hour long, but they use the same technique.

Briefly describe the main plot and the subplot of a television sitcom you have seen recently.

4

Theatrical conventions are the standard practices of drama—the customary way things are done, expected, and accepted by the audience. Three such conventions are:

- *asides*—brief comments made by actors to the audience, unheard by the other actors

- *soliloquy*—a relatively long speech by an actor alone on the stage, directed to the audience or to himself or herself

- *monologue*—a long speech by an actor directed to one or more actors

Think about these conventions, and then write about (a) why a playwright would use them; (b) how they can seem artificial or unlikely; and (c) why the audience easily accepts them anyway.

5

English poetry and drama, including Shakespeare's work, can be analyzed according to the meter, or beat, of words and lines. The repetition of the meter forms a rhythmical pattern. Four common *metric feet* are:

- *iamb*—two syllables, unstressed followed by stressed; example: "destroy"

- *trochee*—two syllables, stressed followed by unstressed; example: "crimson"

- *anapest*—three syllables, two unstressed followed by one stressed; example: "disallow"

- *dactyl*—three syllables, one stressed followed by two unstressed; example: "temperate"

6

In the four columns below, list five words of each type.

iamb	trochee	anapest	dactyl

Iambic pentameter, or five iambs (unstressed then stressed syllables) in a line, has a natural speech rhythm. It has been used by many authors and poets, and was used by Shakespeare for much of the dialogue in his plays.

Write a four-line poem of your own in which each line is written in iambic pentameter. The lines may be rhymed or unrhymed.

Writer's block? Start with the following first line:

"The on/ly thing/ you nev/er said/ to me"

10 syllables

© 2003 J. Weston Walch, Publisher

A playwright uses *foreshadowing* to prepare his audience for what is to come and to heighten anticipation and suspense.

In the space below, draw a symbol or a scene that illustrates the idea of foreshadowing.

8

The practical instructions Shakespeare gave with his plays were few. Stage directions were little more than "Enter," "Exit," and "They fight."

The details of the performance are the work of the *director*. Think of how a printed page comes to life with characters on a stage.

Complete the mind map below by brainstorming all of the duties of a director.

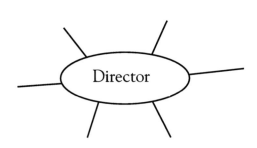

Director

© 2003 J. Weston Walch, Publisher

Shakespeare, and many other writers, used *dramatic irony* in his plays. Also used by the ancient Greeks, dramatic irony creates a situation in which the audience knows what the characters do not know. It is a way of involving the audience in the action as they watch a character fall into a trap they knew was there.

Choose a television sitcom you watch regularly. Describe an episode that includes a situation of dramatic irony.

10

A well-known rival of Shakespeare's, Ben Jonson, praised Shakespeare as a writer "not of an age, but for all time."

Give three reasons why you agree or disagree with Jonson's assessment of Shakespeare.

11

George Gordon Noel Byron, a British poet who lived from 1788 to 1824, said, "Shakespeare's name, you may depend on it, stands absurdly too high and will go down."

Do you agree with this statement? Why or why not? Support your argument with details.

12

For the plots of his plays, Shakespeare often used stories from Greek and Roman mythology, events in English history, or legends from continental Europe. He also "borrowed" the plots of plays that had been written by others. Sometimes these plays were many years old, but occasionally he adapted contemporary pieces. For example, although the story of *Hamlet* comes from an old Danish legend, it already existed in a stage version when Shakespeare took up the story. In fact, some have said that Shakespeare was lucky the concept of plagiarism did not yet exist.

How do you feel about Shakespeare's "borrowing" the ideas of others? Do you feel it lessens his work? In the space below, explain your opinion.

13

Shakespeare was an actor as well as a playwright, and he had a company of actors with whom he worked when developing and writing his plays. Many of the stock characters in his plays, such as his fools or romantic leads, were played by the same actor for several plays in a row. Undoubtedly, the actors had a certain amount of input into what they wanted their characters to say or do, collaborating with the playwright on many aspects of the play during writing and rehearsals.

14

If you went on stage, what kind of character would you want to play? What action would you want to perform—for example, a love scene, a sword fight, or a comic routine? Write a letter to Shakespeare in which you propose your ideas.

Some people argue that Shakespeare could not possibly have written the works that are attributed to him. They point to Shakespeare's limited education as proof that he did not have the knowledge to compose such great works. Some theorize that the work was really written by one of Shakespeare's contemporaries; others suggest that the work was a collaboration of Elizabethan poet-dramatists.

Do you think it matters if Shakespeare was not the true author of the works we ascribe to him? Would we value the works less if they were authored by someone else? Why or why not? Write an essay expressing your opinion below.

15

In some of Shakespeare's plays, characters speak aloud to themselves or they speak directly to the audience. Some television shows and movies use these devices, too. Think about some shows or movies that use these devices (*The Wonder Years* and *Malcolm in the Middle* are just two examples).

What do you think of these devices? What purpose do they serve? Do you enjoy these interruptions in action or not? Write your ideas below, and give reasons for your opinions.

16

Shakespeare used only male actors for performances of his plays. Since there are many female characters in the plays, men or boys would play the female roles.

Why do you think Shakespeare did not use women actors in his performances? If this practice still existed today, how do you think people would feel about it? Discuss your ideas with your classmates.

17

© 2003 J. Weston Walch, Publisher

Many of Shakespeare's comedies include a female character who dresses up as a man to disguise herself for one reason or another. The disguise always leads the character into humorous situations—for example, being challenged to a duel when she has no experience in sword fighting, which is what happens to Viola in *Twelfth Night*. This comic device was a standard gag in Shakespeare's day and was used by many other playwrights.

18

Why do you think audiences of the time found this situation so amusing? Why didn't Shakespeare use the same device for his male characters? (Keep in mind that all of the actors in Shakespeare's day would have been male.) Write a paragraph discussing your ideas below.

The clown is a staple character in Shakespeare's plays. Even in the tragedies, Shakespeare used this character to bring humor into his work. The clown provided comic relief in the form of silly songs and dances, witty remarks or puns, or a view of life from the lower classes. Even today the most dramatic movies, books, television shows, and plays use similar characters to lighten the mood.

Think of two clowns you know of in today's dramas, and compare them to two clowns you know of from Shakespeare's plays. Be sure to provide specific examples.

19

Shakespeare included stock characters—figures who played particular, predictable roles—in his plays. Stock characters include the know-it-all and the clueless parent.

Think about some of the books you have read—including Shakespeare's plays—and movies you have seen. What stock characters seem to continually crop up? List them below, and tell what purpose each serves in the story. Compare your list with those of classmates and look for patterns.

20

Since stages in Shakespeare's time offered little in the way of sophisticated sets or lighting, the actors and the text carried the burden of delivering the drama. In addition, the audience had to imagine what was not represented on the stage.

Think of a current television show. Imagine a scene from that show without props or adequate lighting, and no special effects. What would it be like to view the television performance using just your imagination? Discuss your ideas with your classmates.

21

Compare and contrast a scene from one of Shakespeare's plays with a scene from a modern movie. What special effects would you add to the play? How would this change the performance? Do you think it would enhance the play? Explain why you think so.

22

Choose a character from any of Shakespeare's plays whom you find particularly compelling. Then imagine that you are that character and write several (at least four) diary entries as the character. What does this character observe? What does he or she feel? What are some of the motives and reactions of the character that may not be revealed in the play?

Shakespeare, like other writers and artists of his time, depended upon the patronage, or sponsorship, of a powerful and wealthy person. His plays gained the approval of Queen Elizabeth herself when she saw them at court.

If you were a struggling musician, writer, or artist, to whom would you turn for support and public approval? Write a short letter to your intended patron and explain why he or she should help you.

24

During Shakespeare's time, European society included religion and worship in every part of life. Although there were different religions, they all acknowledged one God. Creation of the universe included a clear structure, with power going from God to kings and their descendants. Each person accepted those above him and below him in status, since God had created it all.

How do you think this structure affected Shakespeare's writing? How is our structure different today?

© 2003 J. Weston Walch, Publisher

Entertainment in Queen Elizabeth's court was, of course, non-electronic. Songs, poems, and dances were created and shared with all. There were elaborate pageants and living pictures called *tableaux vivants*. The ability to compose and perform vocal or instrumental music was part of a noble person's education.

In the space below, write a paragraph about the importance of music in your life and in your society. What is its value? Should it be as basic to public school education as language arts and math? Why?

26

William Shakespeare spent his childhood and early life in a small country town, Stratford-upon-Avon, and went to London later in life to become a playwright.

Take the situation of a small-town actor/writer going to the big city to build a career, and transplant it to today. Write a paragraph or a poem expressing that experience.

27

Shakespeare was known as a playwright by 1592, and by 1594 he was part-owner of a theater company, the Lord Chamberlain's Men. The company built the Globe Theatre in 1599 near the Thames (*tĕmz*) River. The theater was built in the tradition of sports arenas—it was round or octagonal, it had no roof, and audience seats were in covered galleries, similar to bleachers, around the sides. The stage projected into the pit at one end, had a roof, and was open on three sides.

28

Describe the similarities and differences between the Globe Theatre and theaters today.

Shakespeare wrote tragedies, comedies, and histories. Tragedies began around 500 B.C. with the ancient Greeks, who developed stage, actors, and audience from religious ceremonies. The main character in a tragedy falls to ruin because of a character flaw and the influence of higher powers. The audience suffers along with the character and recognizes a profound human experience.

Think about a tragic novel, play, or film you have read or seen. Why is the main character ruined or killed? How is the audience affected? What is to be learned? Why do people like to see such dark dramas?

Write a paragraph about the tragedy you chose.

29

No records document Shakespeare's life from 1585 to 1592 when he was between the ages of 21 and 28. Yet, in his writings, Shakespeare seems to know so much about so many things that it is tempting to speculate about how he supported his young family during this time.

Write a short story discussing his adventures in this time period. Remember, you should be thinking about the subjects of some of his writings and how his experiences would likely contribute to his writings.

30

England of 1592 was an exciting place. The Renaissance, which had begun earlier on the Continent, had reached England. London was becoming a bustling center of commerce; travelers from abroad filled the city; and the country was becoming a powerful nation under its great queen, Elizabeth I.

How did the Renaissance put Shakespeare "in the right place at the right time"? Explain your answer.

Given what you know about the history of England at the time, what particular obstacles or challenges do you think William Shakespeare might have faced as a poet, a playwright, and an actor? Make a list below.

Daily Warm-Ups: Shakespeare

32

Shakespeare wrote many of his plays about political figures before and during his time. Imagine that Shakespeare is alive today. What current events do you think he'd write about? Choose one topic and make notes about his characterization and themes.

Once the Renaissance reached England, the intellectual climate of the day worked to Shakespeare's advantage. People now believed that they had some freedom of choice; they had some part to play in their own destinies. Echoing that belief, Shakespeare wrote in Julius Caesar,

> "The fault, dear Brutus, is not in our stars,
> But in ourselves, that we are underlings."

How has this belief manifested itself in history? Give examples of other writings, documents, speeches, and so on, in which this sentiment is expressed.

34

Queen Elizabeth I loved the theater and arts. She attended stage plays frequently and even paid to see performances.

How do you think the queen's patronage of the arts benefited young playwrights such as William Shakespeare? Do you think that Shakespeare's works would have been famous if it had not been for Queen Elizabeth I? Why or why not? Discuss your ideas with your classmates.

35

Queen Elizabeth I ruled England from 1558 to 1603. Queen Elizabeth II first occupied the English throne in 1952.

What do you know about the interests and accomplishments of Queen Elizabeth I? What do you know about the interests and accomplishments of Queen Elizabeth II? Does she have any characteristics in common with her predecessor? Do you think it would be possible for a current "struggling artist" to gain the favor of Queen Elizabeth II?

36

During Shakespeare's time, stage props were few and lighting was minimal. Sound systems did not exist, of course. Therefore, it was critically important that actors be specially trained and skilled to make their performances memorable.

Given the absence of any technological help, what would be an actor's greatest assets? How is this different from what might be considered the most important assets today? Explain your answers.

During Shakespeare's time in London, the plague killed thousands of people. Lacking scientific knowledge and equipment, people invented reasons for the epidemic. (They did not know the disease was carried by rats' fleas.) Often, magic, the ways of the occult world, folklore, and superstition played a major role in Elizabethan thought.

Try to put yourself in a sixteenth-century frame of mind and write about the reasons for the plague. Include what cures might be effective.

38

During Shakespeare's time, people believed that bad odors caused several diseases, including the plague. Because the plague was so severe in some years in London, the theaters had to be closed.

How do you think this affected Shakespeare himself? What about the theatergoers? How do you think it affected London overall? Share your ideas with your classmates.

39

England might be viewed as the United States' mother country. Write what you know about the history of England and the colonial history of the United States. How does the parent/child metaphor fit this relationship?

40

Shakespeare was a man of the country and was familiar with the fields and forests of his native Stratford. References to flowers and herbs are numerous in his plays.

Write the names of herbs and other plants referenced in his plays; for example, fennel and rosemary. Do some research about these plants on the Internet or at the library. Do the plants supposedly have any medicinal and/or magical properties?

If possible, illustrate the plants you chose.

41

In Shakespeare's time, it was not uncommon for one child in a family to receive a larger inheritance than the other children. Frequently, the oldest son would receive the bulk of his father's wealth and property. In some of Shakespeare's works, this causes tension between siblings. In *As You Like It*, Orlando deeply resents his older brother, Oliver, for treating him unfairly. Oliver wants to destroy his brother so he will not have to share the wealth he inherited.

Daily Warm-Ups: Shakespeare

Do you think the practice of favoring the oldest male child is a fair one? Why or why not? Why might this have been a practical custom in Shakespeare's time? Write an essay stating your opinions below.

42

In 1589–99, the first Globe Theatre was built in London. It may have been the most important structure in Shakespeare's dramatic career. Thousands flocked to the theater to see the works of the up-and-coming playwright. Disapproving of entertainment of any kind, the Puritans closed the Globe in 1642, along with all the playhouses in London. Two years later, the Globe Theatre was torn down.

Imagine you are living in London in 1642. Write an editorial either in support of or in protest against the closing of the Globe Theatre. Include at least three reasons to support your argument.

43

Shakespeare's epitaph on his grave reads:

"Good friend for Jesus sake forbear
To dig the dust enclosed here!
Blest be the man that spares these stones,
And curst be he that moves my bones."

Burial grounds were hard to come by in Shakespeare's time. In many cases, bones were dug up from previous graves to make room for others. Shakespeare was given a plot not because he was a famous actor and playwright, but because he owned land. His bones still remain untouched, though several unsuccessful attempts have been made to open his grave. He is said to be buried 17 feet deep.

44

How do you think the custom of digging up graves to make room for new bodies would affect history? How would our knowledge of Shakespeare change if his grave had been disturbed? Write your ideas below.

Daily Warm-Ups: Shakespeare

Shakespeare wrote many historic plays about political figures of his time. Many have argued that his accounts were inaccurate. Do you think that Shakespeare had a biased view of the figures he wrote about? Why would his plays be inaccurate? Explain your answer.

45

Shakespeare used dramatic language and a variety of poetic devices in his plays.

Match each term with its correct definition.

_____ 1. aside

_____ 2. sonnet

_____ 3. iambic pentameter

_____ 4. soliloquy

a. a speech given by an actor when alone on stage

b. a line of verse/dialogue with ten syllables

c. a 14-line poem using an abab cdcd efef gg rhyme scheme

d. lines spoken outside the hearing of other characters

46

A pun is the humorous use of a word or phrase in which its different meanings are emphasized. Punning appears frequently in Shakespeare's plays and in comedy today. For example, when the generally humorous character Mercutio receives a fatal wound in a duel, he says the following:

"Ask for me tomorrow, and you
shall find me a grave man."

Romeo and Juliet, Act 3, scene 1

Explain the pun. Then find other examples of Shakespeare's puns.

47

Shakespeare wrote his plays in blank verse, which is unrhymed iambic pentameter. That pattern—ten syllables that alternate unstressed and stressed, or five iambs—is widely used because its sound is close to normal English speech.

"I hope/that you/will go/along/with me."

The following lines have five iambs, otherwise known as iambic pentameter:

"I think this tale would win my daughter too."
"Put out the light, and then put out the light."

Othello

"How sweet the moonlight sleeps upon this bank!"

The Merchant of Venice

Copy these three lines below, separating the five iambs with slashes.

A **couplet** **is** **a** **pair** of rhyming lines. The device was frequently used by Shakespeare to neatly sum up and end a scene or an act in a play. Here are some examples:

"For never was a story of more woe
Than this of Juliet and her Romeo."

Romeo and Juliet

"Give me your hands if we be friends,
And Robin shall restore amends."

A Midsummer Night's Dream

Think of a familiar book or film and write a couplet that sums up and ends the story.

49

© 2003 J. Weston Walch, Publisher

Shakespeare's characters

occasionally insult each other in expressive and sometimes graphic words. To invent your own insult using Shakespeare's language, combine one word from each of the three columns below, preceded by the word "Thou." Try to determine what your insult might mean, and then do some research to find out the actual meaning.

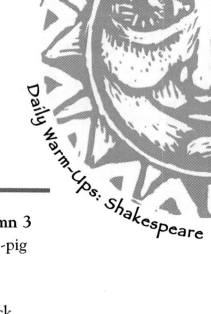

Column 1	Column 2	Column 3
craven	weather-bitten	hedge-pig
mangled	hasty-witted	giglet
unmuzzled	clapper-clawed	varlot
jarring	spur-galled	puttock
wayward	fool-born	baggage
tottering	motley-minded	foot-licker
vain	full-gorged	clack-dish
dankish	urchin-snouted	pumpion
puking	clay-brained	barnacle
goatish	crook-pated	canker-blossom

50

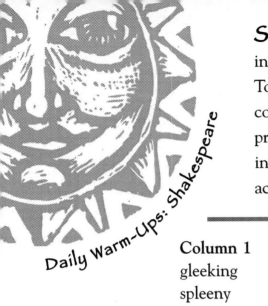

Shakespeare's characters occasionally insult each other in expressive and sometimes graphic words. To invent your own insult using Shakespeare's language, combine one word from each of the three columns below, preceded by the word "Thou." Try to determine what your insult might mean, and then do some research to find out the actual meaning.

Column 1	Column 2	Column 3
gleeking	fly-bitten	measle
spleeny	idle-headed	skainsmate
cockered	flap-mouthed	miscreant
villainous	base-court	pigeon-egg
ruttish	sheep-biting	flax-wench
beslubbering	dizzy-eyed	clotpole
fawning	rude-growing	flap-dragon
surly	onion-eyed	coxcomb
infectious	boil-brained	apple-john
mammering	elf-skinned	haggard

51

Shakespeare's characters occasionally
insult each other in expressive and sometimes graphic words.
To invent your own insult using Shakespeare's language,
combine one word from each of the three columns below,
preceded by the word "Thou." Try to determine what your
insult might mean, and then do some research to find out the
actual meaning.

52

Column 1	Column 2	Column 3
dissembling	guts-griping	joithead
artless	reeling-ripe	nut-hook
churlish	pottle-deep	harpy
fobbing	bat-fowling	maggot-pie
mewling	ill-nurtured	dewberry
rank	pox-marked	boar-pig
weedy	dog-hearted	flirt-gill
paunchy	rough-hewn	bugbear
errant	shard-borne	strumpet
reeky	swag-bellied	bladder

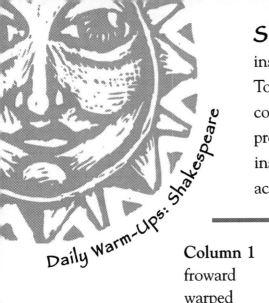

Shakespeare's characters occasionally insult each other in expressive and sometimes graphic words. To invent your own insult using Shakespeare's language, combine one word from each of the three columns below, preceded by the word "Thou." Try to determine what your insult might mean, and then do some research to find out the actual meaning.

Column 1	Column 2	Column 3
froward	knotty-pated	wagtail
warped	fat-kidneyed	bum-bailey
bootless	hell-hated	death-token
gorbellied	tardy-gaited	lewdster
pribbling	dread-bolted	hugger-mugger
droning	beetle-brained	minnow
yeasty	earth-vexing	malt-worm
qualling	dismal-dreaming	codpiece
saucy	common-kissing	fustilarian
roguish	toad-spotted	vassal

53

Shakespeare's characters occasionally

insult each other in expressive and sometimes graphic words. To invent your own insult using Shakespeare's language, combine one word from each of the three columns below, preceded by the word "Thou." Try to determine what your insult might mean, and then do some research to find out the actual meaning.

Column 1	Column 2	Column 3
spongy	folly-fallen	mold-warp
currish	hedge-born	whey-face
bawdy	rump-fed	mumble-news
impertinent	milk-livered	scut
loggerheaded	plume-plucked	horn-beast
clouted	fen-sucked	pignut
lumpish	beef-witted	lout
venomed	ill-breeding	mammet
frothy	tickle-brained	ratsbane
puny	half-faced	gudgeon

54

Advertisements use catchy slogans to get attention and cement a brand name in the minds of potential consumers. Choose one of the quotations from Shakespeare below and use it as part of an advertising campaign for a product. Write your ideas in the form of a radio spot, a script for a television commercial, or copy for a print ad. Then share your ad with classmates.

Out, damned spot!

All that glisters is not gold.

True nobility is exempt from fear.

Old fashions please me most.

The strength of twenty men.

Though this be madness, yet there is method in 't.

Come, give us a taste of your quality.

Of the 17,677 words that Shakespeare used in all of his plays and sonnets, he was the first to use over 1,700 of them. He wrote many of the words and phrases that we consider clichés today. Circle the following words and phrases that you think Shakespeare coined.

Heartsick

One fell swoop

Long-haired

Break the ice

Hot-blooded

Leapfrog

Fancy-free

It's Greek to me

Live-long day

Heart of gold

Foregone conclusion

Naked truth

Strange bedfellows

Eat out of house and home

Dog will have his day

Too much of a good thing

Wear one's heart on one's sleeve

The milk of human kindness

56

Shakespeare was the first to use many of the words we write and speak today in the English language. Some of these words may not have come into use without him. The following is a list of some of the words he was first to write:

gnarled	frugal	bump
countless	lonely	eventful
dwindle	radiance	control
laughable	misplaced	impartial
amazement	obscene	generous
hurry	road	critic

Which of these words do you use most in your daily vocabulary? What would you say instead if Shakespeare had never written these words?

57

In the comedy *As You Like It*, Jaques, a rather unhappy character, says the much-quoted lines "All the world's a stage/And all the men and women merely players."

In this quotation, people are described as "merely" players, or actors. What is the significance of this adjective? What does this suggest about the character's view of the relationship between theater and life? What is your idea of the relationship between theater and life? Write your ideas below.

58

Shakespeare used many literary devices such as metaphors, similes, and allusions. Look at the following lines from *Romeo and Juliet*. Match each literary device with the appropriate line. Then explain each comparison.

_____ 1. "She'll not be hit with Cupid's arrow: She hath Dian's wit,"

_____ 2. "It is the East, and Juliet is the sun!"

_____ 3. " . . . . she hangs upon the cheek of night/Like a rich jewel in an Ethiop's ear—"

a. metaphor

b. simile

c. allusion

A Midsummer Night's Dream is a

Shakespearean comedy frequently read and performed in schools and theater groups.

The play's setting is particularly important, since the time is the summer solstice, or Midsummer Eve. In England, that night was celebrated as the time when supernatural beings caused mischief. The play takes place mostly in an enchanted forest, which is inhabited by fairies.

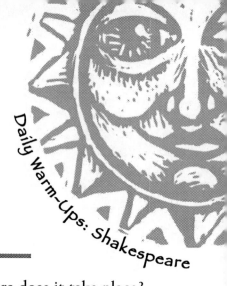

Think about a book you've read recently. When and where does it take place? How does the setting affect the story? Could it have been set elsewhere? Describe an alternate setting.

60

The play *Othello* was based on an Italian novella by Giraldi Cinthio, published in 1565. Shakespeare developed the language, characters, and themes in his own style and for his own purpose. One adaptation he made was to change the character of Othello from a villain to a tragic hero.

Why do you think Shakespeare chose to make that change? Choose a villian from a play, film, or novel you are familiar with. How would you go about changing the villain into a "tragic hero"? Explain your answer.

61

Macbeth, one of Shakespeare's most-performed plays, is the story of the noble lord of Scotland who plots with his wife to kill the king. The king is sleeping trustfully in Macbeth's castle when he is murdered by his host. By the end of Act II, Macbeth has achieved his desire of being the new king.

What do you think happens in the remaining three acts? Imagine what the playwright would say about this ambitious couple. Predict what happens to them. What dramatic possibilities are there? Explain your ideas.

62

Romeo and Juliet is a favorite play of younger students because it tells the story of young lovers. Although Romeo and Juliet's families are feuding with each other, Romeo crashes a party at Juliet's house, wearing a mask to disguise himself.

Masks have been used in many cultures for religious and social reasons. A mask can disguise who you are, but it may also reveal who you want to be.

In the space below, design a mask you would like to wear. Let its details say something about your personality or your desired identity.

63

A **fierce** and longstanding feud between their two families makes Romeo and Juliet's love story complicated and ultimately tragic. The Montagues and Capulets live in the same city and constantly fight with each other. As a result, many characters in the play are killed.

Think about a feud—an ongoing battle—you know about. It might be between individuals or families. Write an essay about how it started and what kept it going. How might it end? What are people really fighting about in a feud?

64

After Romeo and Juliet meet at a party, they meet again in her yard and declare their love for each other. They immediately plan to marry, even though they are both in their early teens and are also well aware that their parents would forbid the marriage.

Imagine that you are Juliet's or Romeo's best friend. She or he tells you about the marriage plan and asks for your help. Write a note to your friend advising him or her on what to do.

65

The *theme* of a story, play, or poem is the central idea being conveyed. It is a truth or a lesson about life and has a general application to all people at all times. A theme of the Cinderella story, for example, might be: "goodness and humility are stronger than cruelty and pride."

Consider the basic facts about the Romeo and Juliet story. Young lovers are secretly married, then forced apart because a feud ignites two murders. A plan backfires, vital information is never delivered, and the two lovers commit suicide. The grieving parents finally make peace at their children's funeral.

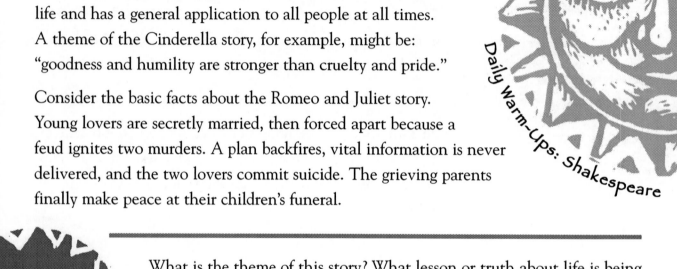

Daily Warm-Ups: Shakespeare

66

What is the theme of this story? What lesson or truth about life is being told? How is this truth still true today? Explain your answers.

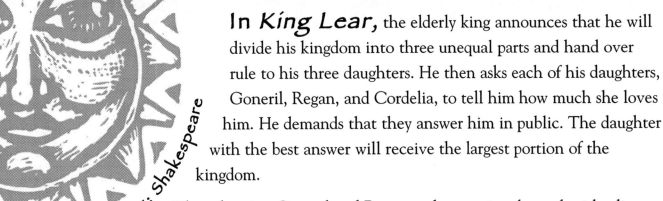

In *King Lear,* the elderly king announces that he will divide his kingdom into three unequal parts and hand over rule to his three daughters. He then asks each of his daughters, Goneril, Regan, and Cordelia, to tell him how much she loves him. He demands that they answer him in public. The daughter with the best answer will receive the largest portion of the kingdom.

The scheming Goneril and Regan make emotional—and misleading—declarations of their love for Lear, but Cordelia, Lear's favorite, refuses to answer, saying only, "I love your majesty according to my bond; nor more nor less." Cordelia is disinherited because she will not flatter her father, even though she really is the daughter who loves him most.

Have you ever been in a position when it would benefit you to flatter a parent rather than tell him or her the truth? Which did you do? Write a paragraph explaining your situation.

In *A Midsummer Night's Dream,*

Demetrius is in love with Hermia, who in turn loves
Lysander. Helena, Hermia's best friend, is in love with
Demetrius. When Hermia runs off with Lysander, Helena tells
Demetrius about their flight in order to win his favor:

> ". . . and for this intelligence
> If I have thanks, it is a dear expense:
> But herein mean I to enrich my pain,
> To have his sight thither and back again."

68

Do you think her plan will work? Would you do the same thing in
her place? Why? Write a letter to Helena explaining what you
think of her plan.

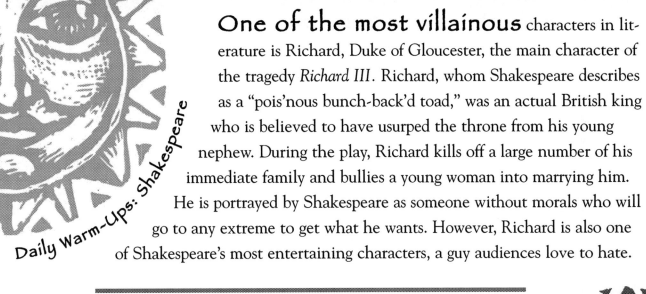

One of the most villainous characters in literature is Richard, Duke of Gloucester, the main character of the tragedy *Richard III*. Richard, whom Shakespeare describes as a "pois'nous bunch-back'd toad," was an actual British king who is believed to have usurped the throne from his young nephew. During the play, Richard kills off a large number of his immediate family and bullies a young woman into marrying him. He is portrayed by Shakespeare as someone without morals who will go to any extreme to get what he wants. However, Richard is also one of Shakespeare's most entertaining characters, a guy audiences love to hate.

Think of other characters from books, television, or movies who are villains but whom audiences love to watch. What do these characters have in common? Why do audiences enjoy watching them so much—even more than watching the "good" characters? Write your ideas below.

69

© 2003 J. Weston Walch, Publisher

The theme of transformation is central to many of Shakespeare's works. The changes experienced by Shakespeare's characters can be physical, emotional, or spiritual. In *As You Like It*, for example, Rosalind dresses and acts as a man to disguise herself. In *King Lear*, the king himself is transformed when he realizes the damage he has done by rejecting his loving daughter, Cordelia.

Have you ever undergone a dramatic transformation in your own life? How did it come about? Are there things about yourself now that you'd like to change? Write a paragraph or poem expressing your ideas.

70

In Shakespeare's *The Tempest*, Prospero is a banished duke stranded on an island with his only daughter, Miranda. Using the magical powers he has developed, he incites a tempest and causes a shipwreck. This introduces a group of new people to the island, including a love interest for his daughter. Throughout the play, Prospero uses his servants and his magical powers to manipulate everyone around him. He is the most powerful character in the play.

It has been said that Prospero is a metaphor for Shakespeare himself. Why might a person come to this conclusion? Do you agree with this analysis? Why or why not?

71

In the very beginning of the tragedy *Romeo and Juliet*, the title characters are called "A pair of star-cross'd lovers." In Shakespeare's time, as well as today, many people believed in fate or destiny. "Star-cross'd" refers to the idea that one's fate is "written in the stars" and cannot be changed.

Besides Romeo and Juliet, can you think of any other star-crossed pairs? These may be real or fictional people, or even groups or organizations. List some doomed pairs below. Then share your list with classmates and tell why you chose these pairs—why they seem destined to a sad fate.

72

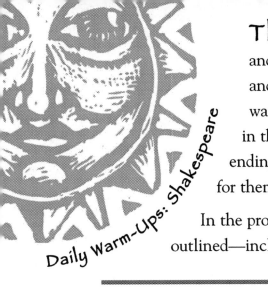

Think about the books you read for pleasure and the movies you can't wait to see. What grabs your interest and keeps it? One reason why many people read books and watch movies is to find out what happens. They are interested in the way the story develops and builds to a climax and ending. Being told the ending beforehand might spoil the story for them.

In the prologue (introduction) to *Romeo and Juliet*, the plot is outlined—including what happens to the title characters.

What do you think of this use of a prologue? What does it suggest about the reasons for watching plays in Shakespeare's day? Write your ideas below.

73

In the tragedy *Macbeth*, Lady Macbeth is tormented by guilt for her role in an assassination by stabbing. This leads her to walk in her sleep and say, "Out, damned spot! out, I say!" while miming washing her hands. She cannot get the imaginary blood stains off her hands.

Think of a story—one you have read or one you make up—in which an object comes to represent, or symbolize, something else. Summarize the story, and describe the symbol, how it affects characters, and what part it plays in the story. Share your scene with classmates.

74

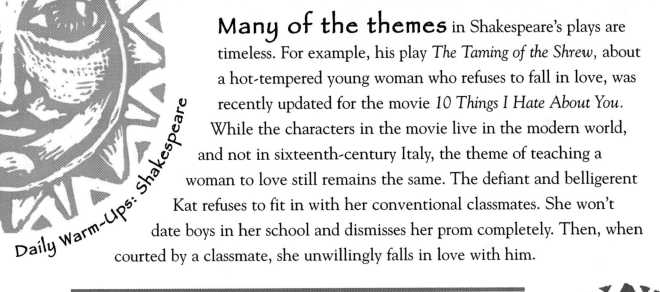

Many of the themes in Shakespeare's plays are timeless. For example, his play *The Taming of the Shrew*, about a hot-tempered young woman who refuses to fall in love, was recently updated for the movie *10 Things I Hate About You*. While the characters in the movie live in the modern world, and not in sixteenth-century Italy, the theme of teaching a woman to love still remains the same. The defiant and belligerent Kat refuses to fit in with her conventional classmates. She won't date boys in her school and dismisses her prom completely. Then, when courted by a classmate, she unwillingly falls in love with him.

Can you think of other books or movies that have a similar theme in which a reluctant woman finally learns to love? Make a list below.

75

In Shakespeare's *Romeo and Juliet*, the theme of young love permeates the play. Although Romeo and Juliet's families are involved in a violent feud, the pair fall in love anyway. They will stop at nothing to be together.

Though times have changed and pre-arranged marriages are not as common as they were in Shakespeare's day, many couples fall in love and cannot be together for various reasons. What might some of these reasons be? Do you think it is right for a couple not to be together if they are in love? Write your ideas below.

76

The theme of jealousy manifests itself throughout *Othello*. In the play, Iago's jealousy of Othello forces him to plot Othello's downfall. Several other characters, including Othello, display jealousy during the play, leading to tragic results. By using such a strong theme, Shakespeare sends the message that jealousy is a deeply evil emotion. Clearly, 400 years later, the same is true today.

List different types of jealousy and what sources they spring from, and then write about which type you think is most destructive and corrupting.

77

Shakespeare chose to write about a character belonging to another race in *Othello*. The main character is a black Moor who is treated as an outsider. Othello's description suggests that he is a black man who comes from central Africa. Few blacks resided in London during Shakespeare's time, and by then the slave trade was well underway. In *Othello*, Shakespeare sympathetically explores how it feels to be an outsider.

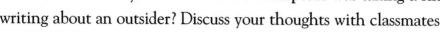

Had Shakespeare written this play in a more racist environment, such as in the South during the U.S. Civil War, how do you think the play would have been received? Do you believe that Shakespeare was taking a risk by writing about an outsider? Discuss your thoughts with classmates.

Daily Warm-Ups: Shakespeare

78

Think about the plot and characters of *Romeo and Juliet*. Do you think these teenagers are more or less restricted than young people their age today? Remember, Juliet is not yet fourteen and Romeo is not much older.

In the space below, make up a chart or diagram that displays the differences in freedom or restrictions between the characters in *Romeo and Juliet* and teenagers today.

79

You are a graphic designer for a theater company, and your latest assignment is a poster for the production of *Romeo and Juliet*. The elements of the play offer exciting possibilities: passionate lovers, savage swordfights, tyrannical parents, a masked ball, a priest, a secret marriage, sleeping potions, daggers, poisons, and tombs.

Sketch the poster below, indcluding the drawings and captions.

80

Shakespeare presented timeless themes—ideas that are as true today as they were when he wrote the plays. That is why his comedies and tragedies have lived on. One of the themes of Shakespeare's *A Midsummer Night's Dream* is "the course of true love never did run smooth."

Think of other plays or novels you have read or movies you have seen that have a similar theme. Brainstorm a list of these works below. Explain in the fewest words possible how the examples illustrate this theme.

81

With a classmate or a small group, choose a scene from one of Shakespeare's plays and act it out.

82

In *Hamlet*, the ghost of Hamlet's father, the previous king of Denmark, appears to Hamlet and tells him that the new king, Hamlet's uncle Claudius, poisoned him in order to get the crown. Hamlet promises the ghost that he will avenge the ghost's murder. Shortly after this appearance, as Hamlet begins to plot his revenge, he decides that he will pretend to go insane: "I perchance hereafter shall think meet to put an antic disposition on."

Hamlet must act out his revenge within a bustling court with many guards and noble people around. Why would it serve Hamlet's purposes to pretend to go mad? Write your answer below.

83

© 2003 J. Weston Walch, Publisher

When his father, the king of Denmark, dies, Hamlet is out of the country at school. By the time he returns, his uncle Claudius has become the new king and has married the queen of the previous king, Hamlet's mother Gertrude.

During the play, it becomes clear that Hamlet is about 30 years old—in other words, old enough and experienced enough to rule as king. Why, then, is Claudius king? With another classmate, brainstorm about how Claudius could become the new king of Denmark under these circumstances.

84

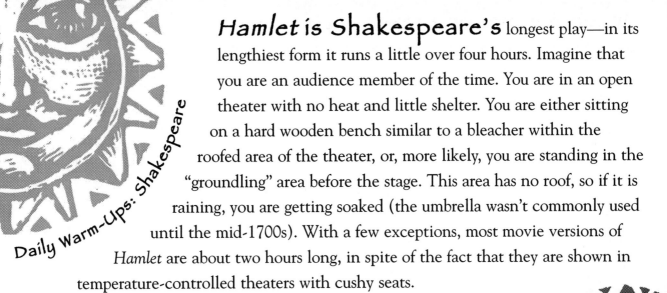

Hamlet is Shakespeare's longest play—in its lengthiest form it runs a little over four hours. Imagine that you are an audience member of the time. You are in an open theater with no heat and little shelter. You are either sitting on a hard wooden bench similar to a bleacher within the roofed area of the theater, or, more likely, you are standing in the "groundling" area before the stage. This area has no roof, so if it is raining, you are getting soaked (the umbrella wasn't commonly used until the mid-1700s). With a few exceptions, most movie versions of *Hamlet* are about two hours long, in spite of the fact that they are shown in temperature-controlled theaters with cushy seats.

Imagine you are talking to a groundling from Shakespeare's time. He has just seen all four hours of *Hamlet* and is ecstatic in his review. Explain to him why a modern audience would be less likely to enjoy the full version of *Hamlet*.

85

In Shakespeare's tragedy, *Hamlet,* the character of Ophelia can be characterized as docile, obedient, and unassertive. Her strict obedience to her father's command ultimately causes her to go mad.

In 1994, a well-known clinical psychologist, Mary Pipher, published a book called *Reviving Ophelia: Saving the Selves of Adolescent Girls.* What do you think the book is about? Why do you think the author chose that title? Explain your answers.

86

Shakespeare's play, *Julius Caesar,* is not so much about the political situation in the Roman Empire as it is about the moral conflicts of its central character. Those moral conflicts are similar to the ones we all face today. Think about these conflicts, and answer the questions below.

What do you do when someone you love or admire is going to do something that you feel is wrong and will hurt others? Are you ever justified in doing something wrong to prevent another from doing something you feel is even more wrong? Explain your answers.

87

Shakespeare was not only a playwright, but also a poet. Following the popular trend of his time, he wrote more than 150 sonnets. Of course, they were so excellent that the form he used has ever since been called the *Shakespearean sonnet*. It has:

- fourteen lines

- three four-line stanzas followed by a rhymed couplet

- a rhyme scheme of *abab cdcd efef gg*

- twelve lines that present an idea or a problem, followed by two lines that finish or solve it

88

In the space below, draw the structure of the Shakespearean sonnet, following the information above. Then indicate the rhyme scheme at the end of the lines.

Here are the first four lines, or quatrain, of Shakespeare's Sonnet 73:

> That time of year thou mayst in me behold
> When yellow leaves, or none, or few, do hang
> Upon those boughs which shake against the cold,
> Bare ruin'd choirs, where late the sweet birds sang.

Read the lines carefully several times, and answer the following:

1. How many syllables are in each line? What is the meter?

2. What is the rhyme scheme (which lines rhyme)?

3. How many sentences are there in the four lines?

4. What is the effect of the three commas in the second line?

5. What is the *metaphor* in these lines (what is compared to what)?

89

Here are the second four lines of Shakespeare's Sonnet 73:

In me thou see'st the twilight of such day
As after sunset fadeth in the west;
Which by and by black night doth take away,
Death's second self, that seals up all in rest.

1. What is the reader asked to "see" in the speaker?

2. What is "Death's second self"?

3. How many kinds of "rest" are implied?

4. Where are there examples of *alliteration* (repeated consonants placed close together in a line)?

90

Here are lines 9 through 12, the third quatrain, in Shakespeare's Sonnet 73:

> In me thou see'st the glowing of such fire,
> That on the ashes of his youth doth lie,
> As the death-bed whereon it must expire,
> Consumed with that which it was nourisht by.

---

1. What is the central *metaphor* of these lines?

2. Draw a picture of the metaphor below.

3. *Paraphrase*, or put in your own words, the thoughts of this section of the poem.

91

Shakespeare's sonnets have as their subjects love, friendship, good and bad fortune, time, and death.

Try writing at least one quatrain in Shakespeare's form: four lines, iambic pentameter (ten syllables in a line), rhyming lines 1 and 3, and 2 and 4 (abab).

Write about one of the subjects listed above.

92

The following lines are the first 12 lines from Shakespeare's Sonnet 25. Since you know that the last two lines of his sonnets, called a rhyming couplet, sum up the previous 12 lines, what do you think the rhyming couplet for this sonnet will be? Write the last two lines of the sonnet. Then find Shakespeare's rhyming couplet. Compare your version to Shakespeare's.

Let those who are in favour with their stars
Of public honour and proud titles boast,
Whilst I, whom fortune of such triumph bars
Unlook'd for joy in that I honour most.
Great princes' favourites their fair leaves spread
But as the marigold at the sun's eye,
And in themselves their pride lies buried,
For at a frown they in their glory die.
The painful warrior famoused for fight,
After a thousand victories once foiled,
Is from the book of honour razed quite,
And all the rest forgot for which he toiled:

93

The following lines are the first 12 lines from Shakespeare's Sonnet 54. Since you know that the last two lines of his sonnets, called a rhyming couplet, sum up the previous 12 lines, what do you think the rhyming couplet for this sonnet will be? Write the last two lines of the sonnet. Then find Shakespeare's rhyming couplet. Compare your version to Shakespeare's.

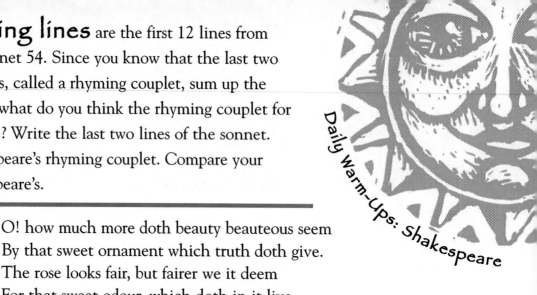

94

O! how much more doth beauty beauteous seem
By that sweet ornament which truth doth give.
The rose looks fair, but fairer we it deem
For that sweet odour, which doth in it live.
The canker blooms have full as deep a dye
As the perfumed tincture of the roses,
Hang on such thorns, and play as wantonly
When summer's breath their masked buds discloses:
But, for their virtue only is their show,
They live unwoo'd, and unrespected fade;
Die to themselves. Sweet roses do not so;
Of their sweet deaths are sweetest odours made:

The following is Shakespeare's Sonnet 36. Read it, and then discuss the theme throughout the sonnet. How does the final couplet change in attitude? Write your ideas below.

Let me confess that we two must be twain,
 Although our undivided loves are one;
  So shall these blots that do with me remain,
  Without thy help, by me be borne alone.
In our two loves there is but one respect,
Though in our lives a separable spite,
Which though it alter not love's sole effect,
Yet doth it steal sweet hours from love's delight.
I may not evermore acknowledge thee,
Lest my bewailed guilt should do thee shame;
Nor thou with public kindness honour me,
Unless though take that honour from thy name:
  But do not so; I love thee in such sort,
  As, thou being mine, mine is thy good report.

95

© 2003 J. Weston Walch, Publisher

Below is Shakespeare's Sonnet 116. After

reading it, answer the following questions: What is the overall theme of the poem? What is the tone of the poem?

Let me not to the marriage of true minds
Admit impediments. Love is not love
Which alters when it alteration finds
Or bends with the remover to remove.
O, no! It is an ever-fixed mark
That looks on tempests and is never shaken.
It is the star to every wand'ring bark,
Whose worth's unknown, although his heighth be taken.
Love's not Time's fool, though rosy lips and cheeks
Within his bending sickle's compass come.
Love alters not with his brief hours and weeks,
But bears it out even to the edge of doom.
   If this be error and upon me proved,
   I never writ, nor no man ever loved.

Below is a sonnet by Elizabeth Barrett Browning called "How Do I Love Thee?" Read the sonnet and then compare it to the Shakespearean sonnets that you know. How are they alike? How are they different? Write your answers below.

How do I love thee? Let me count the ways.
I love thee to the depth and breadth and height
My soul can reach, when feeling out of sight
For the ends of Being and ideal Grace.
I love thee to the level of everyday's
Most quiet need, by sun and candle-light.
I love thee freely, as men strive for Right;
I love thee purely, as they turn from Praise.
I love thee with the passion put to use
In my old griefs, and with my childhood's faith.
I love thee with a love I seemed to lose
With my lost saints,—I love thee with the breath,
Smiles, tears, of all my life!—and, if God choose,
I shall but love thee better after death.

97

© 2003 J. Weston Walch, Publisher

Memorize one of Shakespeare's sonnets. Recite it, and illustrate a poster that graphically depicts the poem. Sketch the poster below.

98

Choose one of Shakespeare's love sonnets. Write it in a letter and send it to someone special.

99

Could not take truce with the unruly
spleen/Of Tybalt deaf to peace . . .

Romeo and Juliet, Act 3, scene 1

What do you think the word *spleen* means in this quotation?

Rewrite the lines, substituting another word or words for *spleen*.

100

God in heaven bless her! You are to blame, my lord, to **rate** her so.

Romeo and Juliet, Act 3, scene 5

What do you think the word *rate* means? Rewrite the lines, substituting another word or words for *rate*.

© 2003 J. Weston Walch, Publisher

For I have need of many **orisons** to move the heavens to smile upon my state.

Romeo and Juliet, Act 4, scene 1

What do you think the word *orisons* means? Rewrite the line, substituting another word or words for *orisons*.

102

All this I know and to the marriage her nurse
is **privy.**

Romeo and Juliet, Act 5, scene 3

What do you think the word *privy* means? Rewrite the line,
substituting another word or words for *privy*.

103

Give every man thine ear, but few thy voice.

Hamlet, Act 1, scene 3

Read the line above and think about what it means. Then rewrite the line in your own words.

104

Your horrid image doth unfix my hair.

Macbeth, Act 1, scene 3

Read the line above and think about what it means. Then rewrite the line in your own words.

105

© 2003 J. Weston Walch, Publisher

Take every man's censure, but reserve thy judgment.

Hamlet, Act 1, scene 3

Read the line above and think about what it means. Then rewrite the line in your own words.

106

Friends, Romans, countrymen, lend me your ears.

Julius Caesar, Act 3, scene 2

Read the line above and think about what it means. Then rewrite the line in your own words.

There can be no kernel in this light nut; the soul of this man is his clothes.

All's Well That Ends Well, Act 2, scene 5

Read the line above and think about what it means. Then rewrite the line in your own words.

108

There is occasions and causes why and wherefore in all things.

Henry V, Act 5, scene 1

Read the line above and think about what it means. Then rewrite the line in your own words.

Daily Warm-Ups: Shakespeare

109

In a false quarrel there is no true valor.

Much Ado About Nothing, Act 5, scene 1

Read the line above and think about what it means. Then rewrite the line in your own words.

110

After he scores he never pays the score.

All's Well That Ends Well, Act 4, scene 3

Read the line above and think about what it means. Then rewrite the line in your own words.

111

Conscience does make cowards of us all.

Hamlet, Act 3, scene 1

Read the line above and think about what it means. Then rewrite the line in your own words.

112

Every why hath a wherefore.

The Comedy of Errors, Act 2, scene 2

Read the line above and think about what it means. Then rewrite the line in your own words.

113

Things sweet to taste prove in digestion sour.

Richard II, Act 1, scene 3

Read the line above and think about what it means. Then rewrite the line in your own words.

114

He has everything that an honest man should not have; what an honest man should have, he has nothing.

All's Well That Ends Well, Act 4, scene 3

Read the line above and think about what it means. Then rewrite the line in your own words.

You whose grossness little characters sum up.

Troilus and Cressida, Act 1, scene 3

Read the line above and think about what it means. Then rewrite the line in your own words.

116

Men shut their doors against a setting sun.

Timon of Athens, Act 1, scene 2

Read the line above and think about what it means. Then rewrite the line in your own words.

He that dies pays all debts.

The Tempest, Act 3, scene 2

Read the line above and think about what it means. Then rewrite the line in your own words.

Daily Warm-Ups: Shakespeare

118

Wilt thou show the whole wealth of thy wit in an instant?

Merchant of Venice, Act 3, scene 5

Read the line above and think about what it means. Then rewrite the line in your own words.

By medicine life may be prolonged, yet death will seize the doctor too.

Cymbeline, Act 5, scene 5

Read the line above and think about what it means. Then rewrite the line in your own words.

120

The tempter or the tempted, who sins most?

Measure for Measure, Act 2, scene 2

Read the line above and think about what it means. Then rewrite the line in your own words.

121

Thy words, I grant, are bigger; for I wear not my dagger in my mouth.

Cymbeline, Act 4, scene 2

Read the line above and think about what it means. Then rewrite the line in your own words.

122

Your face is as a book where men may read strange matters.

Macbeth, Act 1, scene 5

Read the line above and think about what it means. Then rewrite the line in your own words.

All that glisters is not gold.

The Merchant of Venice, Act 2, scene 7

Read the line above and think about what it means. Then rewrite the line in your own words.

124

There is nothing either good or bad, but thinking makes it so.

Hamlet, Act 2, scene 2

Read the line above and think about what it means. Then rewrite the line in your own words.

No legacy is so rich as honesty.

All's Well That Ends Well, Act 3, scene 5

Read the line above and think about what it means. Then describe a person (famous, known to you, or fictional) who might say such a thing, and explain why he or she might say it.

126

I wasted time, and now doth time waste me.

Richard II, Act 5, scene 5

Read the line above and think about what it means. Then describe a person (famous, known to you, or fictional) who might say such a thing, and explain why he or she might say it.

127

We know what we are, but not what we may be.

Hamlet, Act 4, scene 5

Read the line above and think about what it means. Then describe a person (famous, known to you, or fictional) who might say such a thing, and explain why he or she might say it.

128

Words pay no debts.

Troilus and Cressida, Act 3, scene 2

Read the line above and think about what it means. Then describe a person (famous, known to you, or fictional) who might say such a thing, and explain why he or she might say it.

129

I must be cruel, only to be kind.

Hamlet, Act 3, scene 4

Read the line above and think about what it means. Then describe a person (famous, known to you, or fictional) who might say such a thing, and explain why he or she might say it.

130

Daily Warm-Ups: Shakespeare

The miserable have no other medicine but only hope.

Measure for Measure, Act 3, scene 1

Read the line above and think about what it means. Then describe a person (famous, known to you, or fictional) who might say such a thing, and explain why he or she might say it.

131

Heat not a furnace for your foe so hot that it do singe yourself.

Henry VIII, Act 1, scene 1

Read the line above and think about what it means. Then describe a person (famous, known to you, or fictional) who might say such a thing, and explain why he or she might say it.

132

I will speak daggers to her.

Hamlet, Act 3, scene 2

Read the line above and think about what it means. Then describe a person (famous, known to you, or fictional) who might say such a thing, and explain why he or she might say it.

She does abuse to our ears.

All's Well That Ends Well, Act 5, scene 3

Read the line above and think about what it means. Then describe a person (famous, known to you, or fictional) who might say such a thing, and explain why he or she might say it.

134

There's no more valor in him than in a wild duck.

1 Henry IV, Act 2, scene 2

Read the line above and think about what it means. Then describe a person (famous, known to you, or fictional) who might say such a thing, and explain why he or she might say it.

135

© 2003 J. Weston Walch, Publisher

He has not so much brain as ear wax.

Troilus and Cressida, Act 5, scene 1

Read the line above and think about what it means. Then describe a person (famous, known to you, or fictional) who might say such a thing, and explain why he or she might say it.

136

Thou prunest a rotten tree.

As You Like It, Act 2, scene 3

Read the line above and think about what it means. Then describe a person (famous, known to you, or fictional) who might say such a thing, and explain why he or she might say it.

137

Though it makes the unskillful laugh, it cannot but make the judicious grieve.

Hamlet, Act 3, scene 2

Read the line above and think about what it means. Then describe a person (famous, known to you, or fictional) who might say such a thing, and explain why he or she might say it.

138

Daily Warm-Ups: Shakespeare

Love all, trust a few.

All's Well That Ends Well, Act 1, scene 1

Read the line above and think about what it means. Then describe a person (famous, known to you, or fictional) who might say such a thing, and explain why he or she might say it.

How bitter a thing it is to look into happiness through another man's eyes!

As You Like It, Act 5, scene 2

Read the line above and think about what it means. Then describe a person (famous, known to you, or fictional) who might say such a thing, and explain why he or she might say it.

140

Cowards die many times before their deaths;
The valiant never taste of death but once.

Julius Caesar, Act 2, scene 2

Read the line above and think about what it means. Then describe a person (famous, known to you, or fictional) who might say such a thing, and explain why he or she might say it.

Nature teaches beasts to know their friends.

Coriolanus, Act 2, scene 1

Read the line above and think about what it means. Then describe a person (famous, known to you, or fictional) who might say such a thing, and explain why he or she might say it.

142

The course of true love never did run smooth.

A Midsummer Night's Dream, Act 1, scene 1

Read the line above and think about what it means. Then describe a person (famous, known to you, or fictional) who might say such a thing, and explain why he or she might say it.

143

O, that this too, too solid flesh would melt, thaw and resolve itself into a dew.

Hamlet, Act 1, scene 2

Read the line above and think about what it means. Then describe a situation in which such a thing might be said, and explain why someone might say it.

144

Wisely and slow. They stumble that run fast.

Romeo and Juliet, Act 2, scene 2

Read the line above and think about what it means. Then describe a situation in which such a thing might be said, and explain why someone might say it.

145

Happy are they that hear their detractions and can put them to mending.

Much Ado About Nothing, Act 2, scene 3

Read the line above and think about what it means. Then describe a situation in which such a thing might be said, and explain why someone might say it.

146

What's done cannot be undone. To bed, to bed, to bed.

Macbeth, Act 5, scene 1

Read the line above and think about what it means. Then describe a situation in which such a thing might be said, and explain why someone might say it.

147

© 2003 J. Weston Walch, Publisher

Misery acquaints a man with strange bedfellows.

The Tempest, Act 2, scene 2

Read the line above and think about what it means. Then describe a situation in which such a thing might be said, and explain why someone might say it.

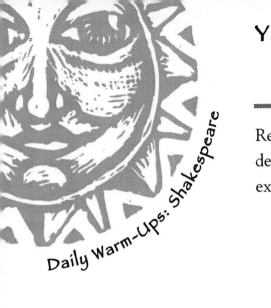

Your mind is tossing on the ocean.

The Merchant of Venice, Act 1, scene 1

Read the line above and think about what it means. Then describe a situation in which such a thing might be said, and explain why someone might say it.

149

You are a vagabond and no true traveler.

All's Well That Ends Well, Act 2, scene 3

Read the line above and think about what it means. Then describe a situation in which such a thing might be said, and explain why someone might say it.

150

Nothing in his life became him like the leaving it.

Macbeth, Act 1, scene 4

Read the line above and think about what it means. Then describe a situation in which such a thing might be said, and explain why someone might say it.

© 2003 J. Weston Walch, Publisher

To show an unfelt sorrow is an office which the false man does easy.

Macbeth, Act 2, scene 3

Read the line above and think about what it means. Then describe a situation in which such a thing might be said, and explain why someone might say it.

152

Neither a borrower, nor a lender be; For loan oft loses both itself and friend.

Hamlet, Act 1, scene 3

Read the line above and think about what it means. Then describe a situation in which such a thing might be said, and explain why someone might say it.

© 2003 J. Weston Walch, Publisher

This above all: to thine own self be true.

Hamlet, Act 1, scene 3

Read the line above and think about what it means. Then describe a situation in which such a thing might be said, and explain why someone might say it.

154

Some are born great, some achieve greatness, and some have greatness thrust upon them.

Twelfth Night, Act 2, scene 5; Act 3, scene 4

Read the line above and think about what it means. Then describe a situation in which such a thing might be said, and explain why someone might say it.

© 2003 J. Weston Walch, Publisher

Better three hours too soon than minute too late.

The Merry Wives of Windsor, Act 2, scene 2

Read the line above and think about what it means. Then describe a situation in which such a thing might be said, and explain why someone might say it.

156

Rich gifts wax poor when givers prove unkind.

Hamlet, Act 3, scene 1

Read the line above and think about what it means. Then describe a situation in which such a thing might be said, and explain why someone might say it.

157

Ill blows the wind that profits nobody.

3 Henry VI, Act 2, scene 5

Read the line above and think about what it means. Then describe a situation in which such a thing might be said, and explain why someone might say it.

158

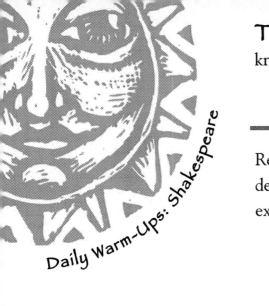

The fool doth think he is wise, but the wise man knows himself to be a fool.

As You Like It, Act 5, scene 1

Read the line above and think about what it means. Then describe a situation in which such a thing might be said, and explain why someone might say it.

Our doubts are traitors, and make us lose the good we oft might win, by fearing to attempt.

Measure for Measure, Act 1, scene 4

Read the line above and think about what it means. Then describe a situation in which such a thing might be said, and explain why someone might say it.

160

Daily Warm-Ups: Shakespeare

Brevity is the soul of wit.

Hamlet, Act 2, scene 2

Read the line above and think about what it means. Then describe a person (famous, known to you, or fictional) to whom you would like to say these words.

The devil can cite scripture for his purpose.

The Merchant of Venice, Act 1, scene 3

Read the line above and think about what it means. Then describe a person (famous, known to you, or fictional) to whom you would like to say these words.

162

It is a wise father that knows his own child.

The Merchant of Venice, Act 2, scene 2

Read the line above and think about what it means. Then describe a person (famous, known to you, or fictional) to whom you would like to say these words.

163

Sweet flowers are slow and weeds make haste.

Richard III, Act 2, scene 4

Read the line above and think about what it means. Then describe a person (famous, known to you, or fictional) to whom you would like to say these words.

Daily Warm-Ups: Shakespeare

164

I do desire we may be better strangers.

As You Like It, Act 3, scene 2

Read the line above and think about what it means. Then describe a person (famous, known to you, or fictional) to whom you would like to say these words.

© 2003 J. Weston Walch, Publisher

O Beware, my lord, of jealousy; it is the green-ey'd monster which doth mock the meat it feeds on.

Othello, Act 3, scene 3

Read the line above and think about what it means. Then describe a person (famous, known to you, or fictional) to whom you would like to say these words.

166

They do not love that do not show their love.

Two Gentlemen of Verona, Act 1, scene 2

Read the line above and think about what it means. Then describe a person (famous, known to you, or fictional) to whom you would like to say these words.

I am a kind of burr; I shall stick.

Measure for Measure, Act 4, scene 3

Read the line above and think about what it means. Then describe a person (famous, known to you, or fictional) to whom you would like to say these words.

168

An honest tale speeds best, being plainly told.

Richard III, Act 4, scene 4

Read the line above and think about what it means. Then describe a person (famous, known to you, or fictional) to whom you would like to say these words.

O! It is excellent to have a giant's strength; but it is tyrannous to use it like a giant.

Measure for Measure, Act 2, scene 2

Read the line above and think about what it means. Then describe a person (famous, known to you, or fictional) to whom you would like to say these words.

170

A crafty knave needs no broker.

2 Henry VI, Act 1, scene 2

Read the line above and think about what it means. Then describe a person (famous, known to you, or fictional) to whom you would like to say these words.

171

A little pot is soon hot.

The Taming of the Shrew, Act 4, scene 1

Read the line above and think about what it means. Then describe a person (famous, known to you, or fictional) to whom you would like to say these words.

172

If your girdle should break, how would thy guts fall about thy knees.

1 Henry IV, Act 3, scene 3

Read the line above and think about what it means. Then describe a person (famous, known to you, or fictional) to whom you would like to say these words.

© 2003 J. Weston Walch, Publisher

Your face is not worth sunburning.

Henry V, Act 5, scene 2

Read the line above and think about what it means. Then describe a person (famous, known to you, or fictional) to whom you would like to say these words.

Daily Warm-Ups: Shakespeare

174

© 2003 J. Weston Walch, Publisher

Your mount would trot as well were some of your brags dismounted.

Henry V, Act 3, scene 7

Read the line above and think about what it means. Then describe a person (famous, known to you, or fictional) to whom you would like to say these words.

© 2003 J. Weston Walch, Publisher

Let's meet as little as we can.

As You Like It, Act 3, scene 2

Read the line above and think about what it means. Then
describe a person (famous, known to you, or fictional) to
whom you would like to say these words.

176

Daily Warm-Ups: Shakespeare

There's many a man hath more hair than wit.

The Comedy of Errors, Act 2, scene 2

Read the line above and think about what it means. Then describe a person (famous, known to you, or fictional) to whom you would like to say these words.

177

Thou hast neither heat, affection, limb nor beauty to make thy riches pleasant.

Measure for Measure, Act 3, scene 1

Read the line above and think about what it means. Then describe a person (famous, known to you, or fictional) to whom you would like to say these words.

178

You speak an infinite deal of nothing.

The Merchant of Venice, Act 1, scene 1

Read the line above and think about what it means. Then describe a person (famous, known to you, or fictional) to whom you would like to say these words.

© 2003 J. Weston Walch, Publisher

Better a witty fool than a foolish wit.

Twelfth Night, Act 1, scene 5

Read the line above and think about what it means. Then describe a person (famous, known to you, or fictional) to whom you would like to say these words.

180

Background

1. Responses will vary. Students may complain about unfair restrictions and so on. This is an opportunity to point out those reasons why Shakespeare's work has lasted while today's popular entertainment will not.
2. *As You Like It*—comedy
   Romeo and Juliet—tragedy
   King Richard III—history
3. The best answer is 5, because it incorporates all of the other choices and is a reflection of Shakespeare's versatility.

4–23. Answers will vary.

History

24–45. Answers will vary.

Shakespeare's Language

46. aside—d
    sonnet—c
    iambic pentameter—b
    soliloquy—a

47. Answers will vary.
48. "I think/ this tale/ would win/ my daugh/ter too."
    "Put out/ the light,/ and then/ put out/ the light."
    "How sweet/ the moon/light sleeps/ upon/ this bank!"

49–55. Answers will vary.
56. All words and phrases should be circled.
57–58. Answers will vary.
59. 1. allusion
    2. metaphor
    3. simile

Themes

60–87. Answers will vary.

Sonnets

88. Answers will vary. Check students' diagrams.
89. 1. 10; iambic pentameter
    2. abab
    3. one

Daily Warm-Ups: Shakespeare

4. The commas force the speaker's voice to pause, emphasizing the last few leaves.
5. The poet's age is compared to autumn.

90. 1. twilight of the day and the poet
2. "night"
3. the rest of night and the rest of death
4. <u>b</u>y and <u>b</u>y <u>b</u>lack" and "<u>s</u>econd <u>s</u>elf, that <u>s</u>eals"

91. 1. The poet's age is compared to a dying fire.
2. Pictures will vary.
3. Answers will vary.

92. Answers will vary.

93. "Then happy I, that love and am beloved, Where I may not remove nor be removed." Students' couplets will vary.

94. "And so of you, beauteous and lovely youth, When that shall vade, my verse distills your truth." Students' couplets will vary.

95–96. Answers will vary.

97. Answers will vary, but students should notice the difference in rhyme scheme.

98–99. Answers will vary.

Quotations: Use Your Own Words

100. emotional, angry temper
101. abuse
102. prayers
103. in on a secret
104–125. Answers will vary.

Quotations: Characterization

126–143. Answers will vary.

Quotations: Motivation

144–160. Answers will vary.

Quotations: Words to Speak to Someone

161–180. Answers will vary.

Turn downtime into learning time!

Other books in the

Daily *Warm-Ups* series:

- Algebra
- Analogies
- Biology
- Critical Thinking
- Earth Science
- Geography
- Geometry
- Journal Writing

- Poetry
- Pre-Algebra
- Spelling & Grammar
- Test-Prep Words
- U.S. History
- Vocabulary
- World History
- Writing